Owls

Adult Coloring Book

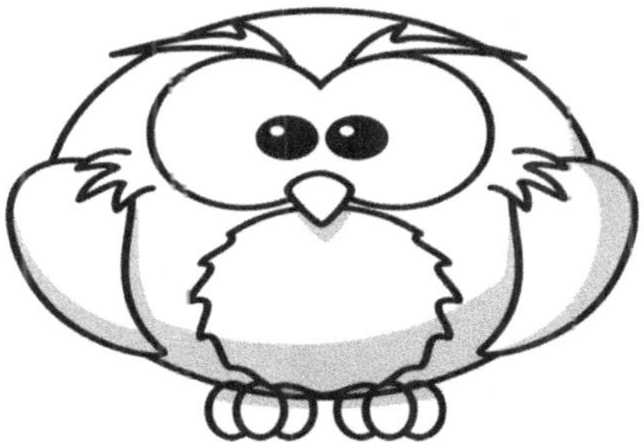

The Creativity Tree

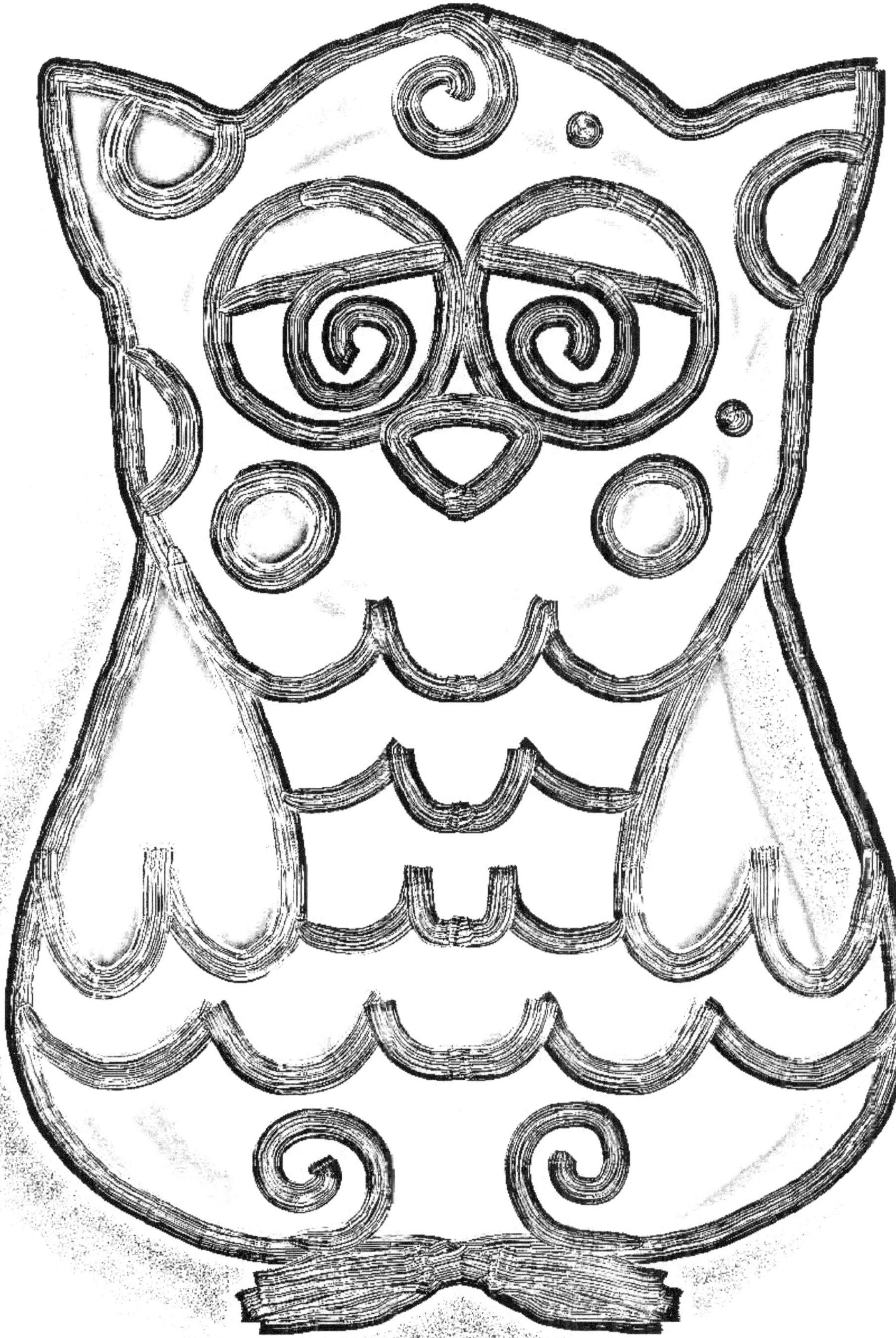

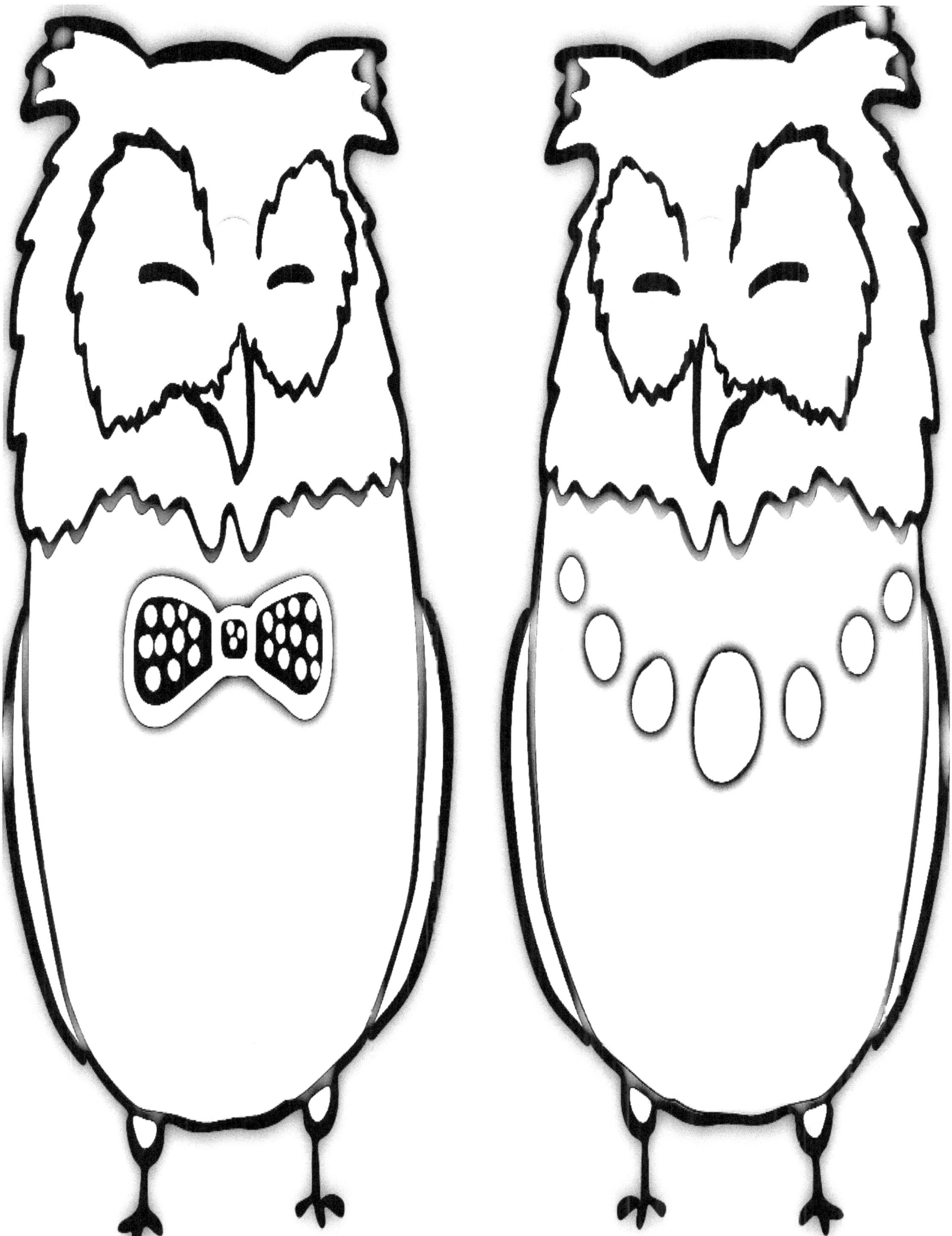

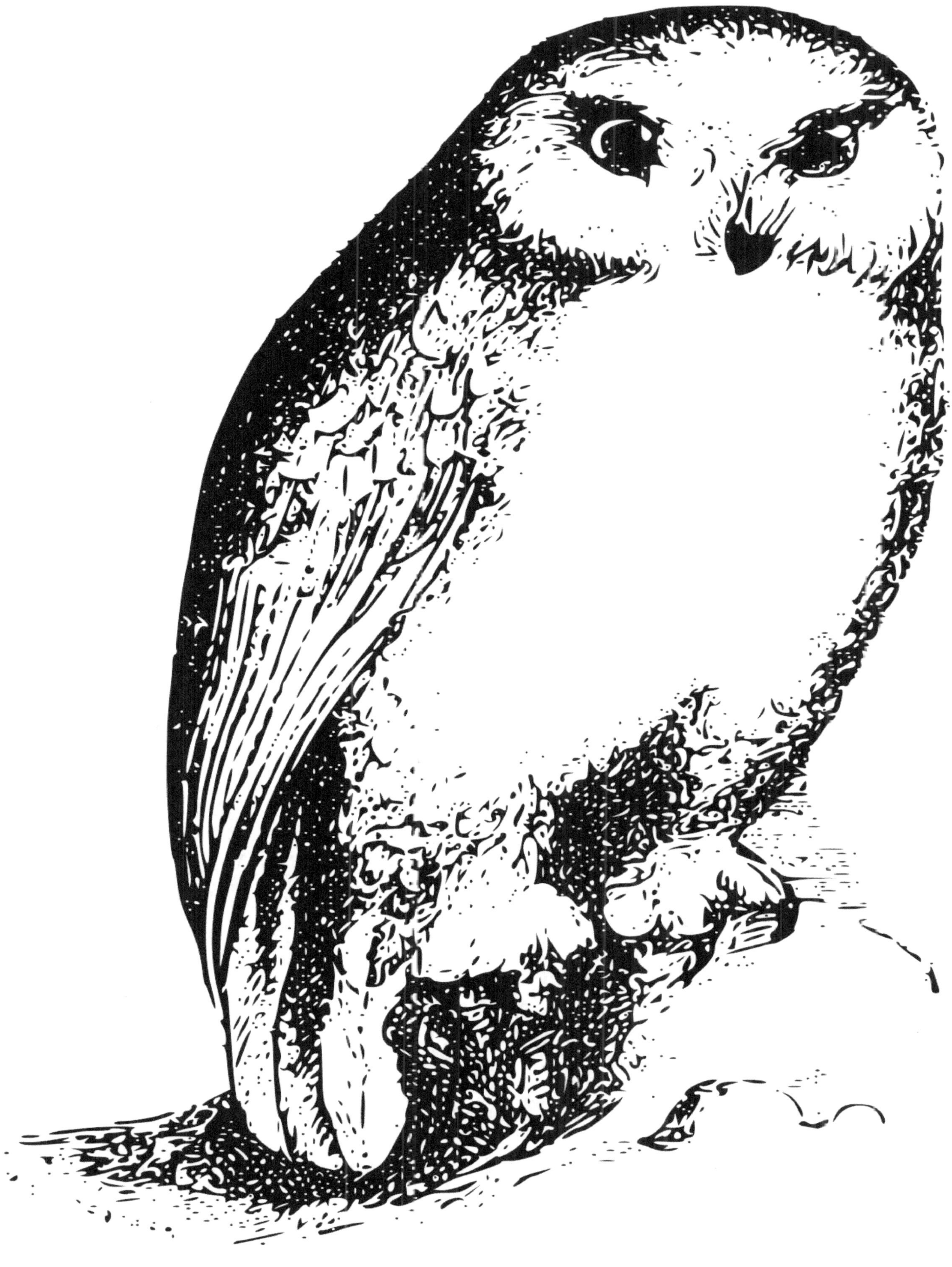

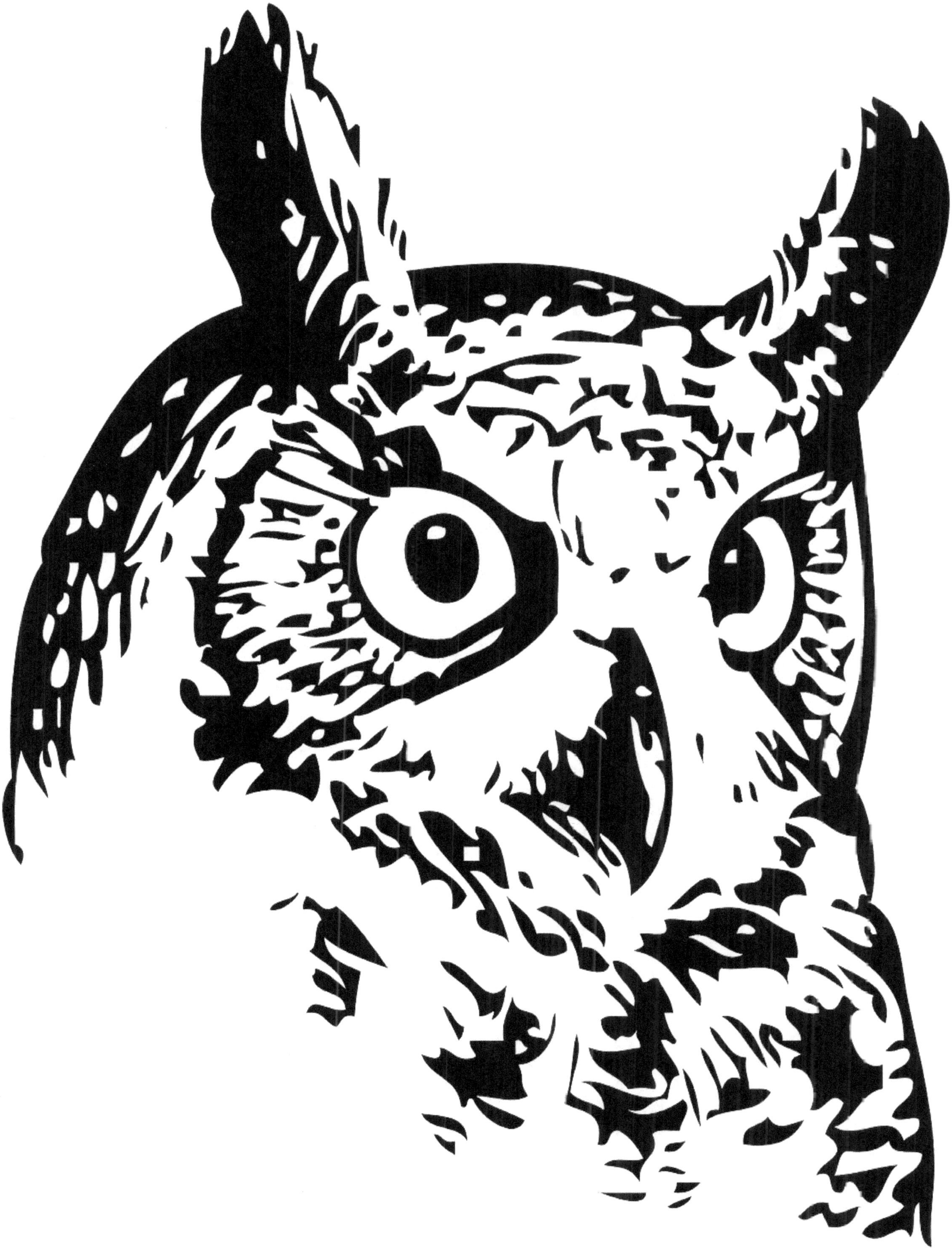

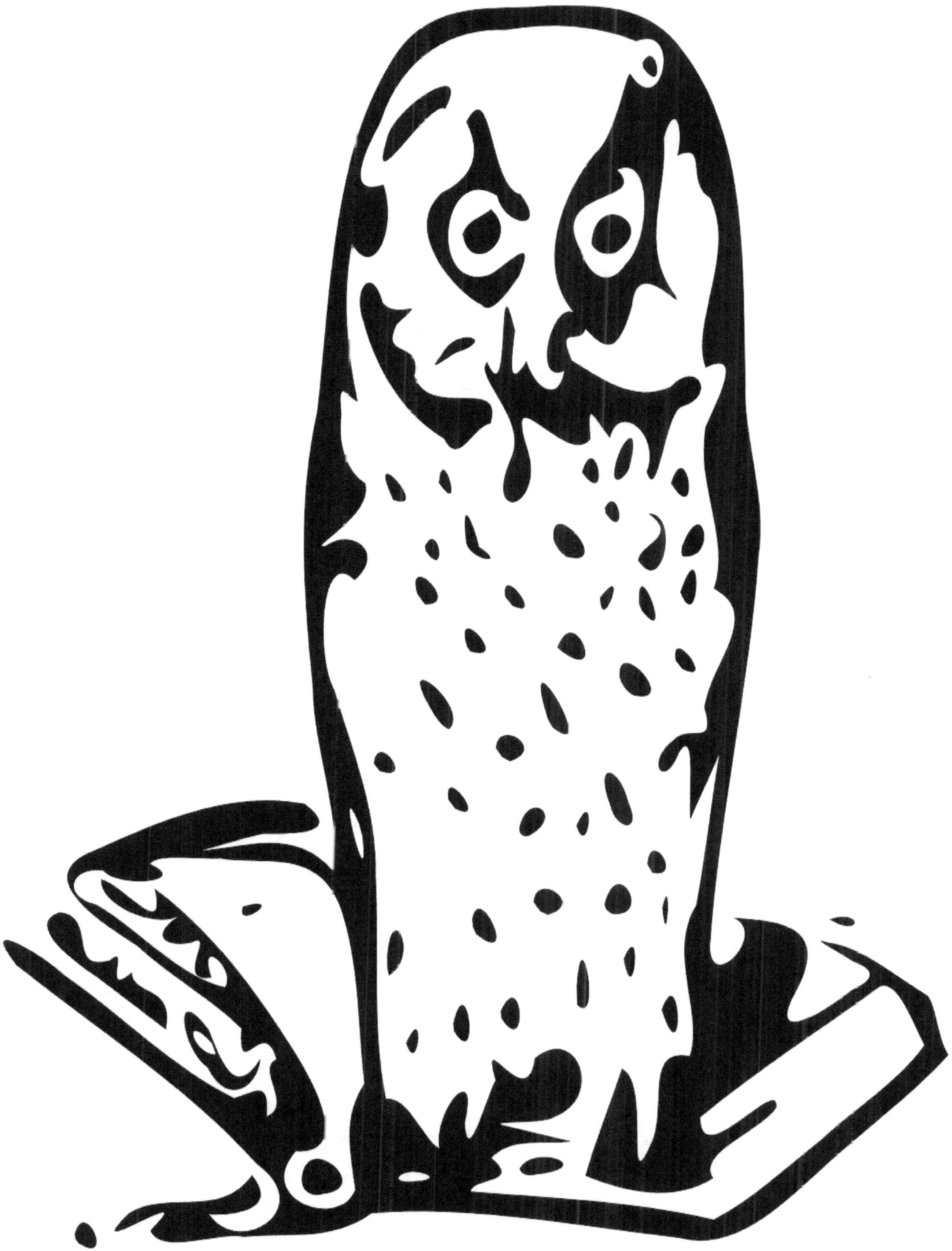

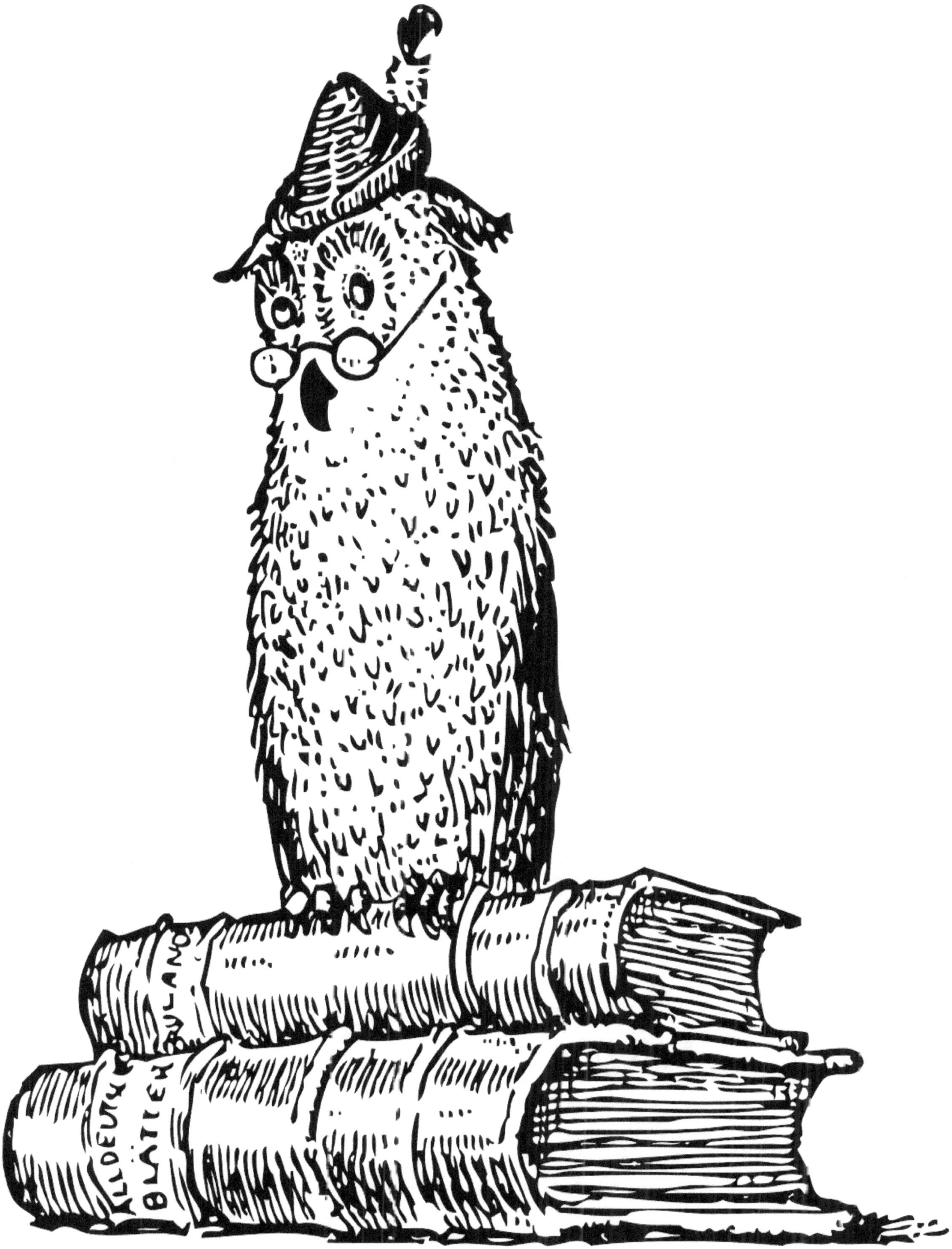

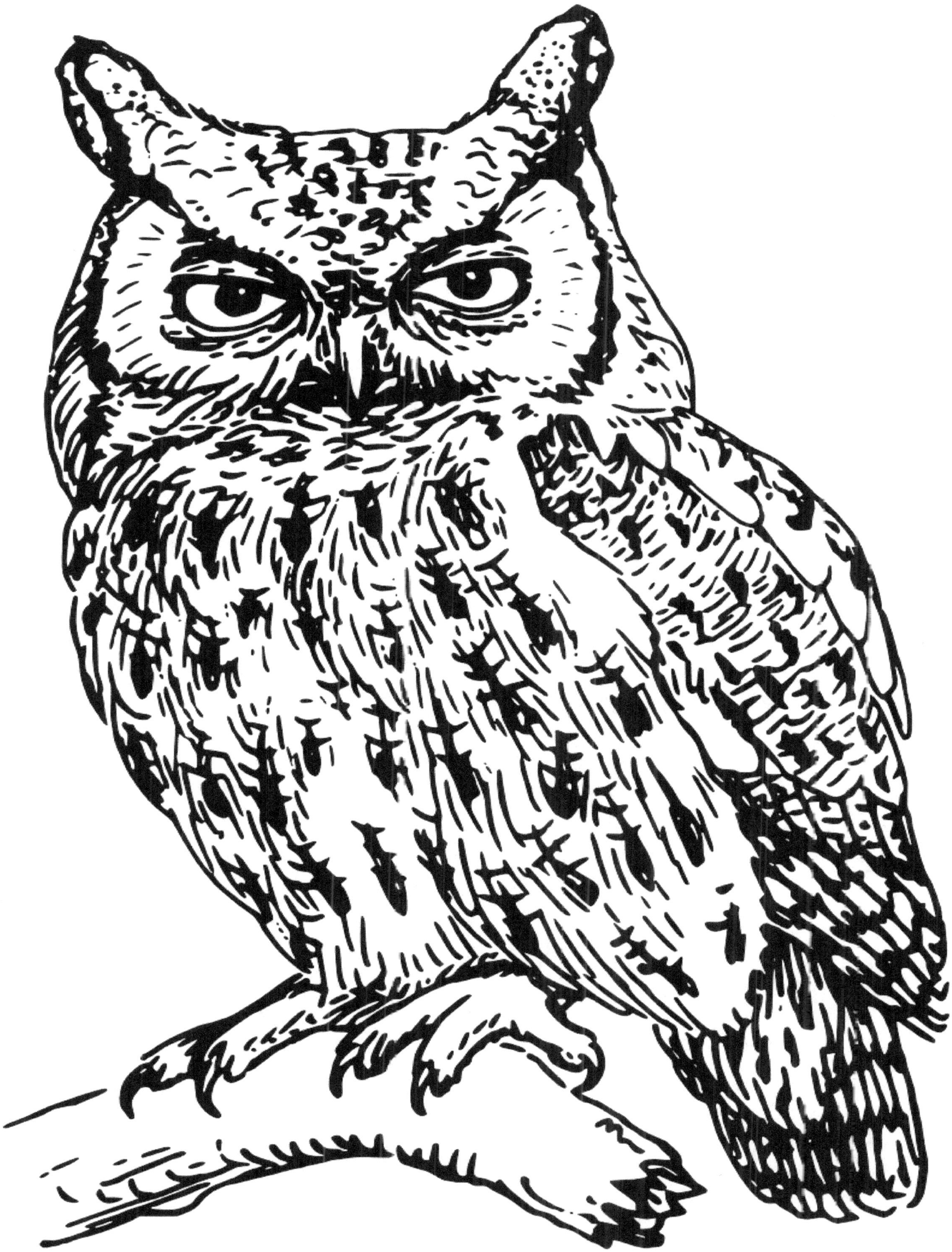

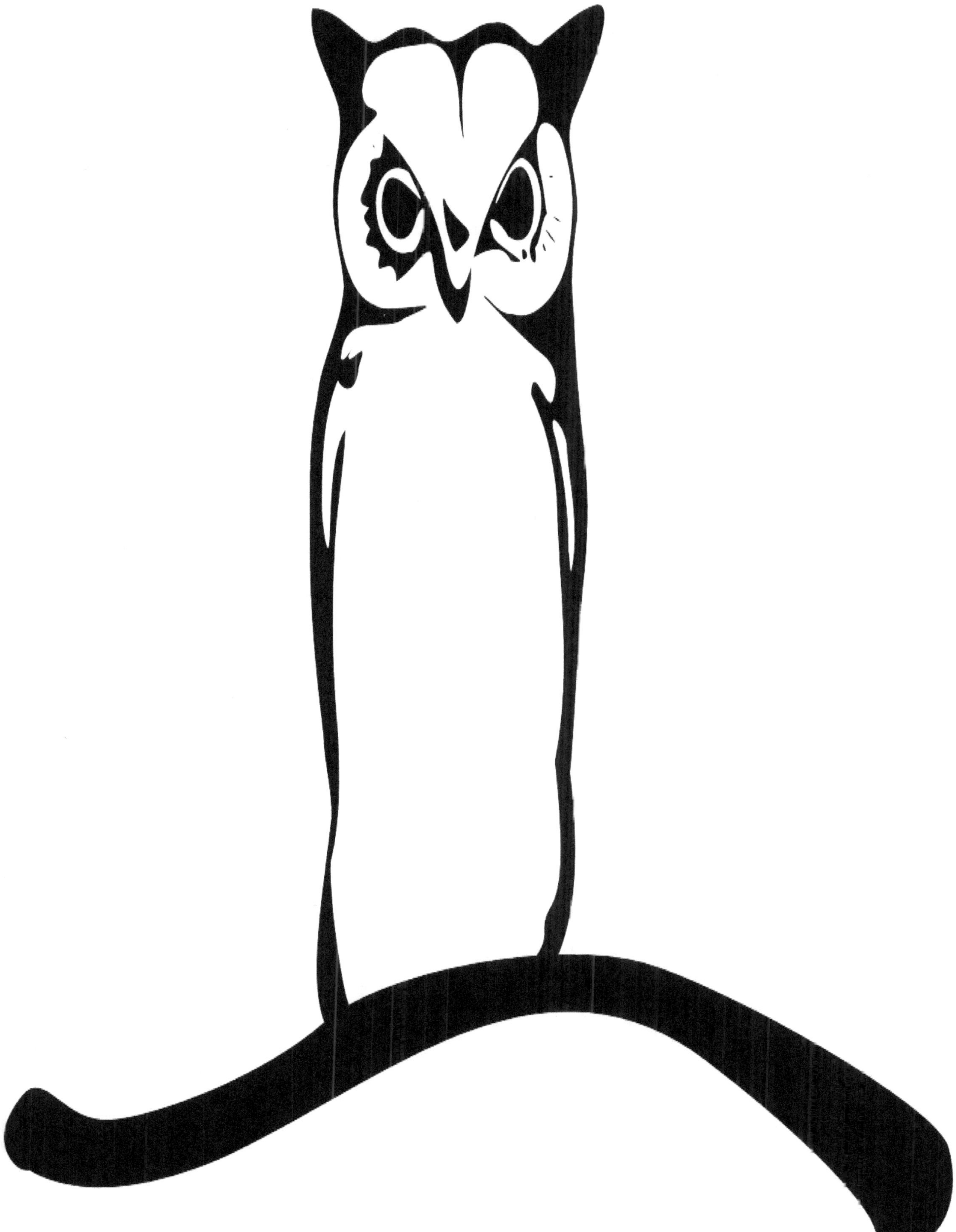

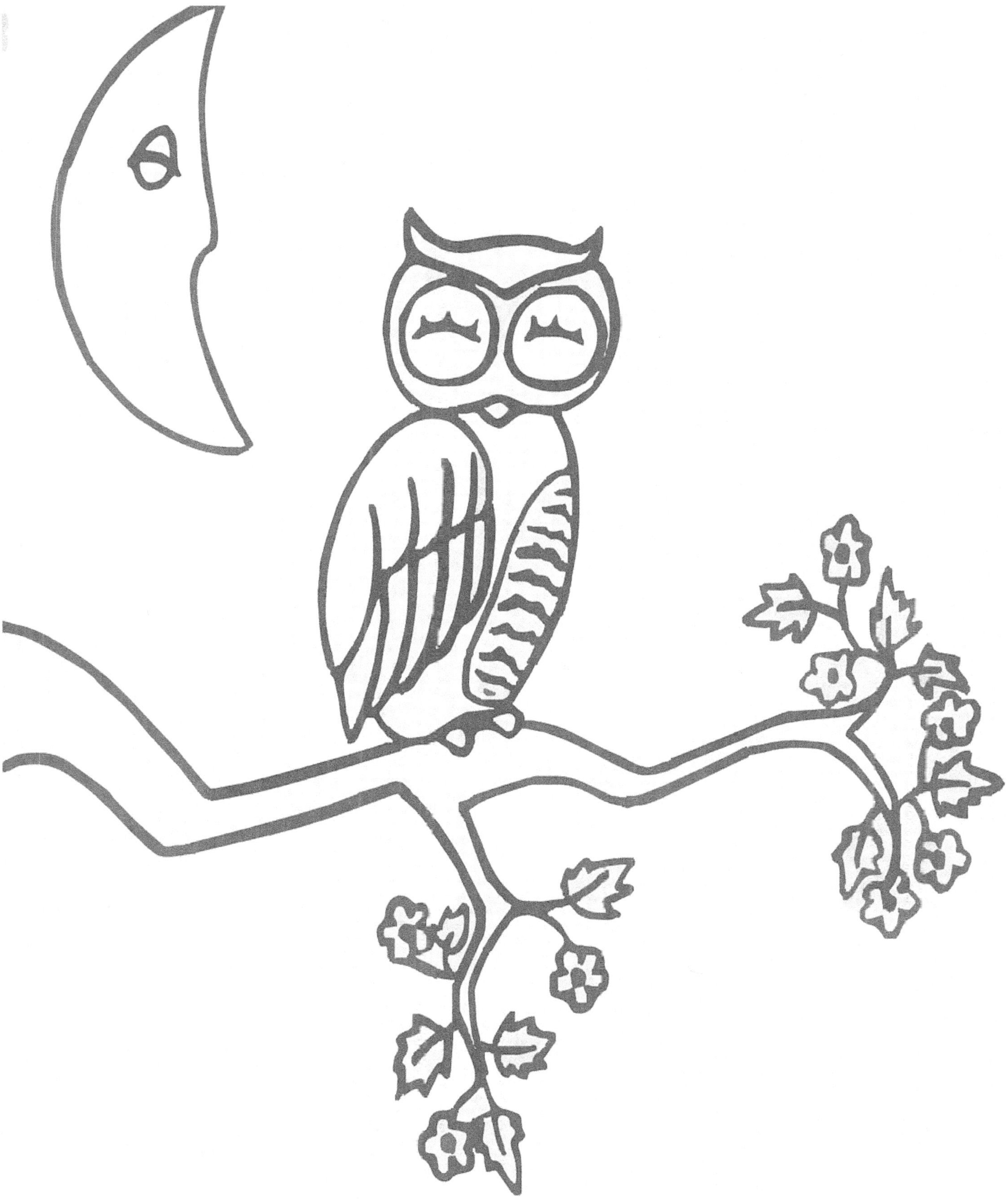

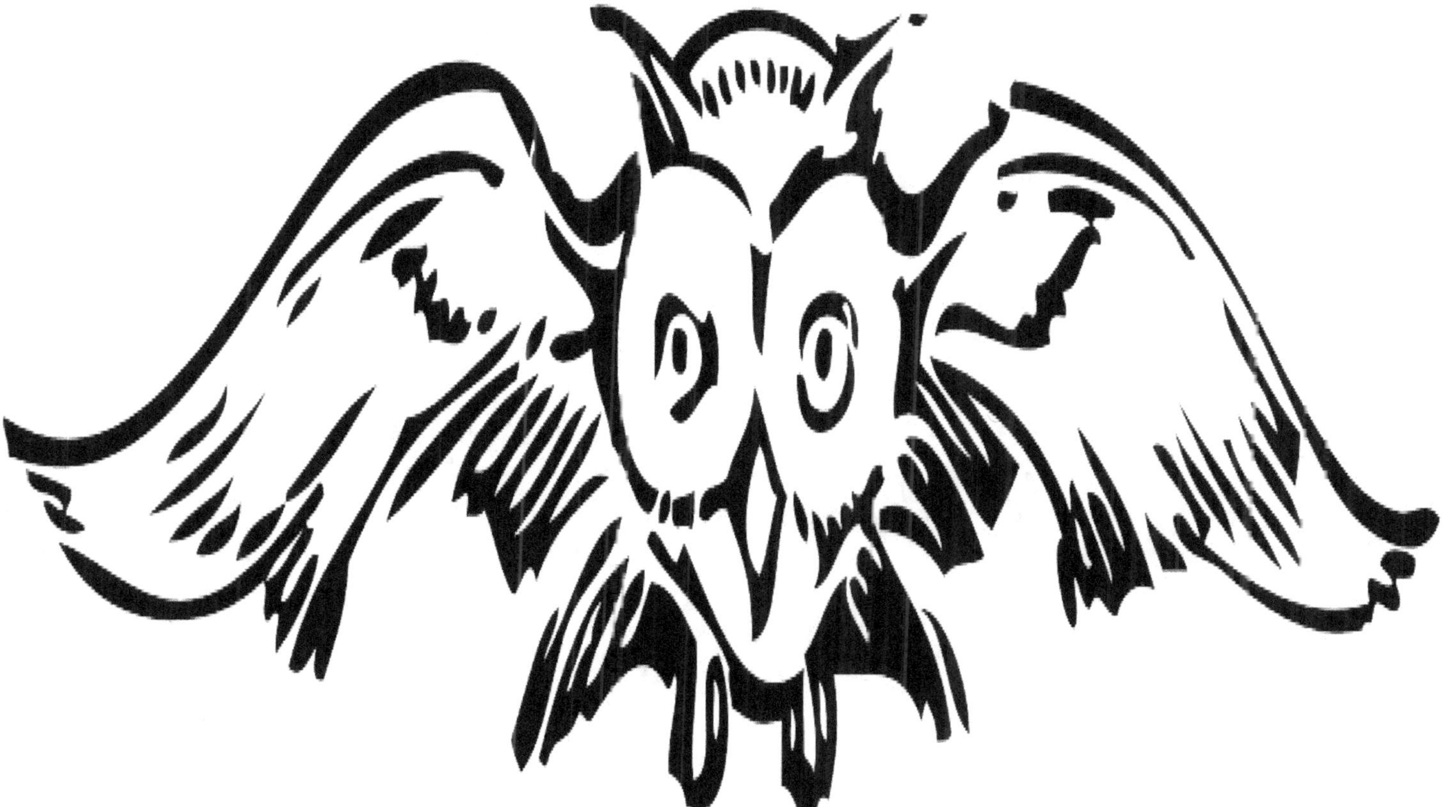

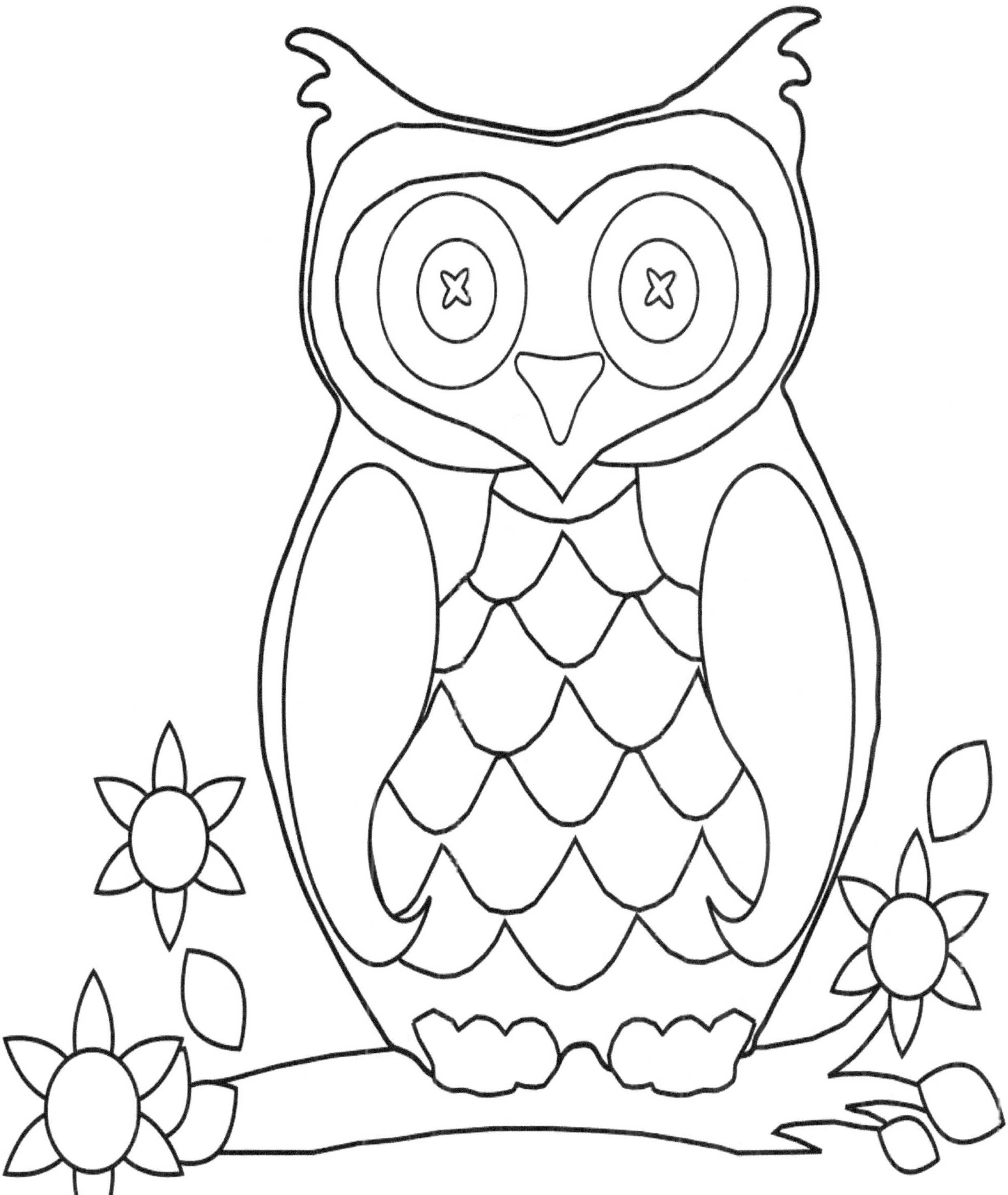

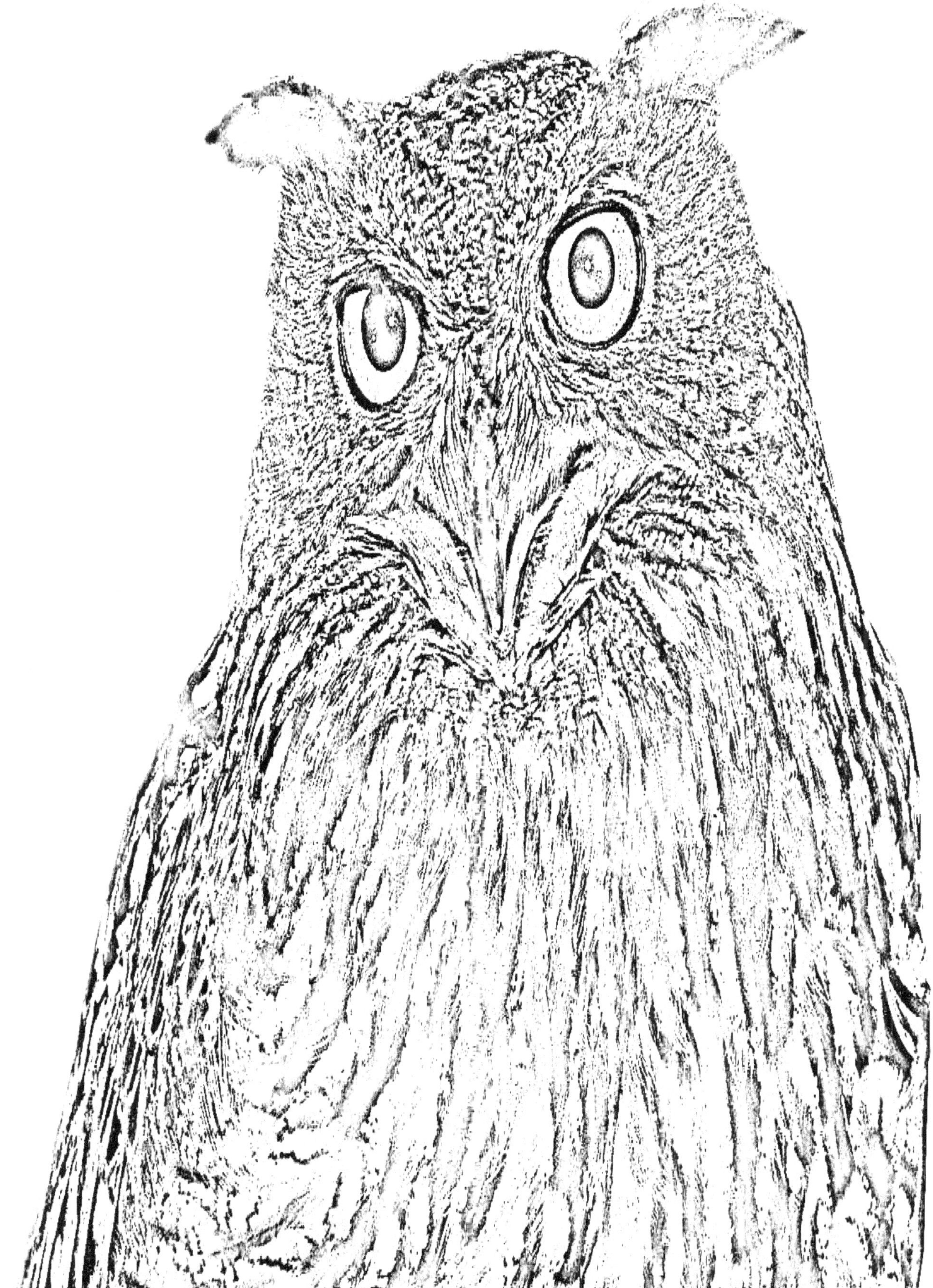

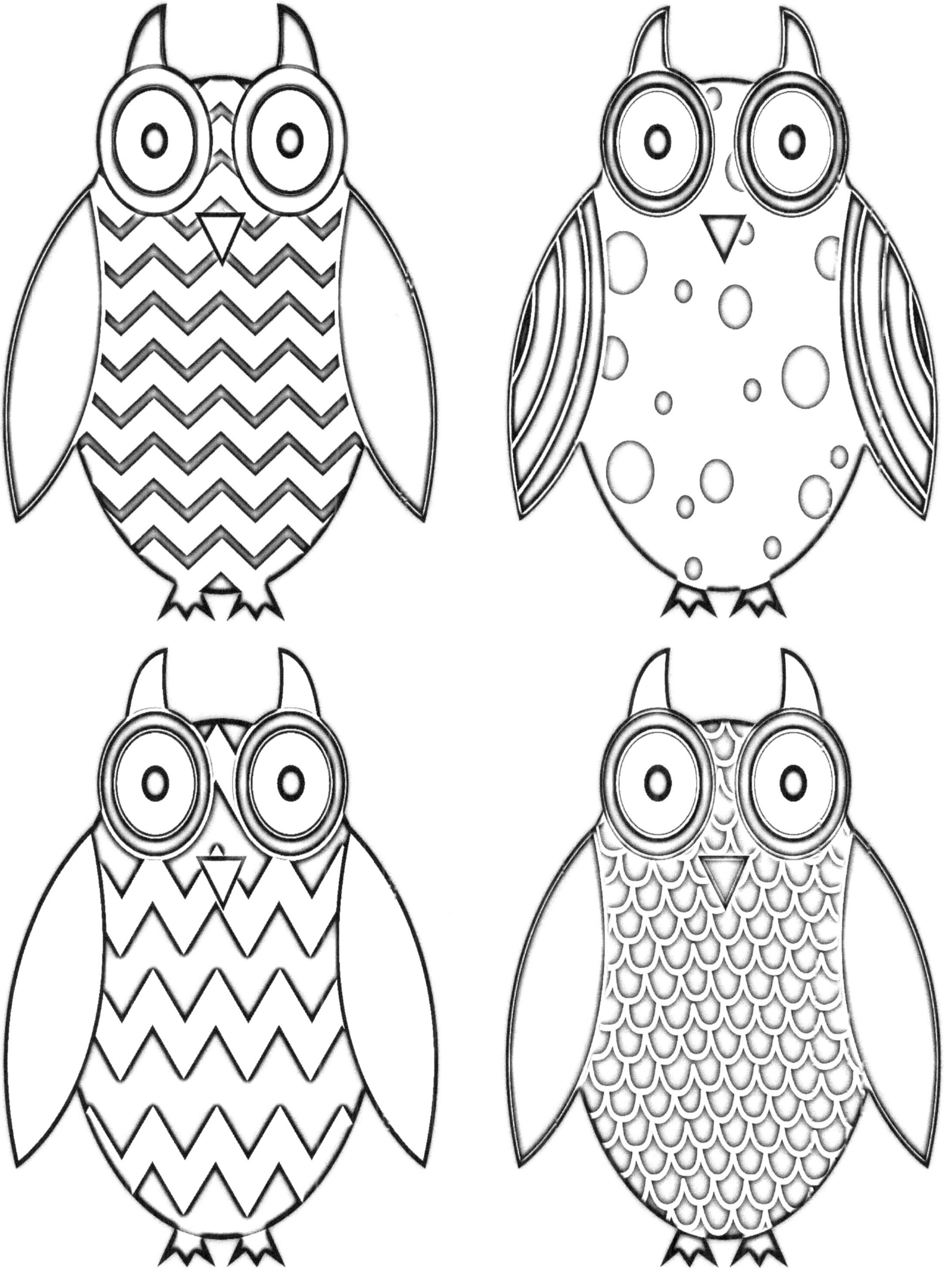

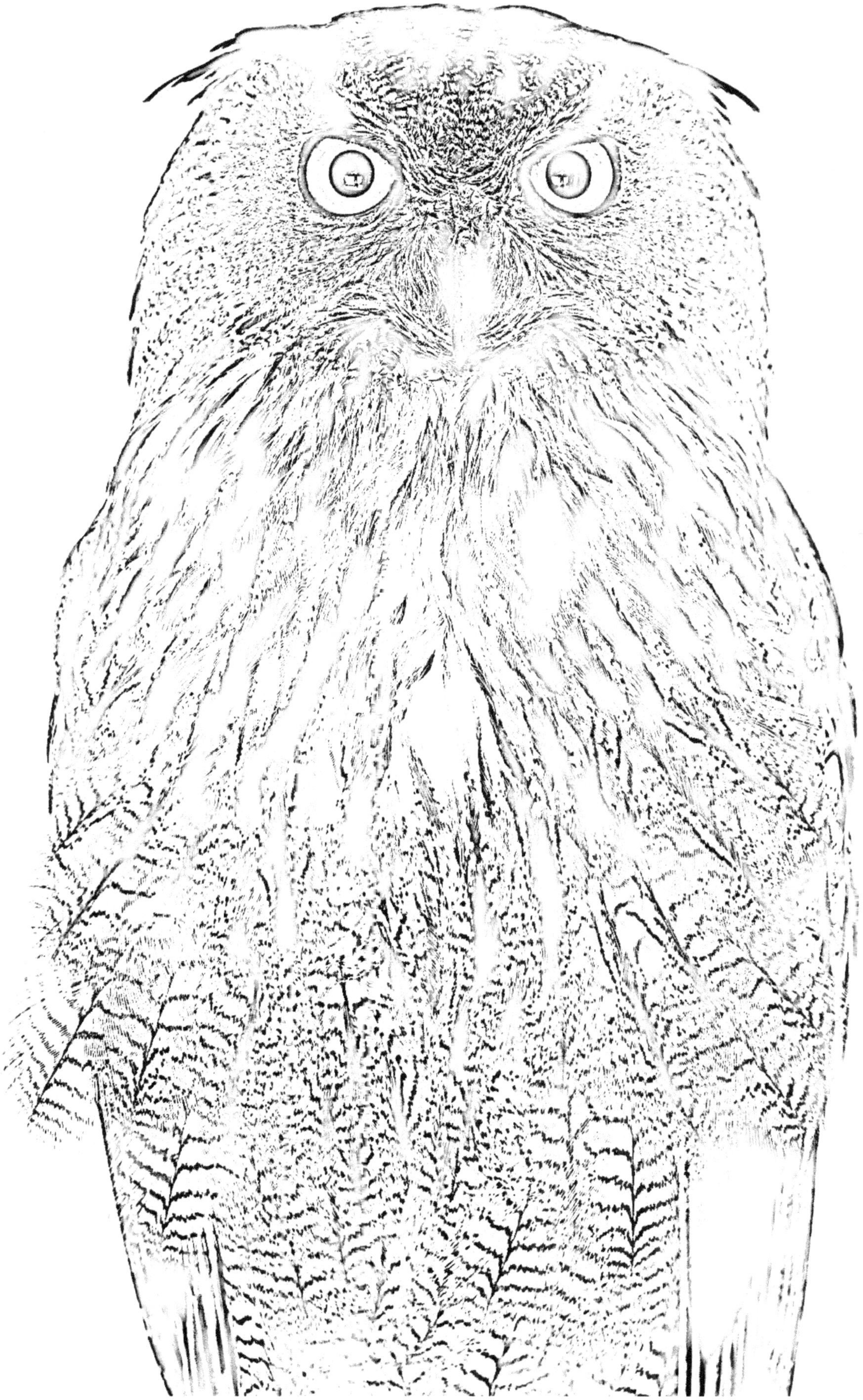

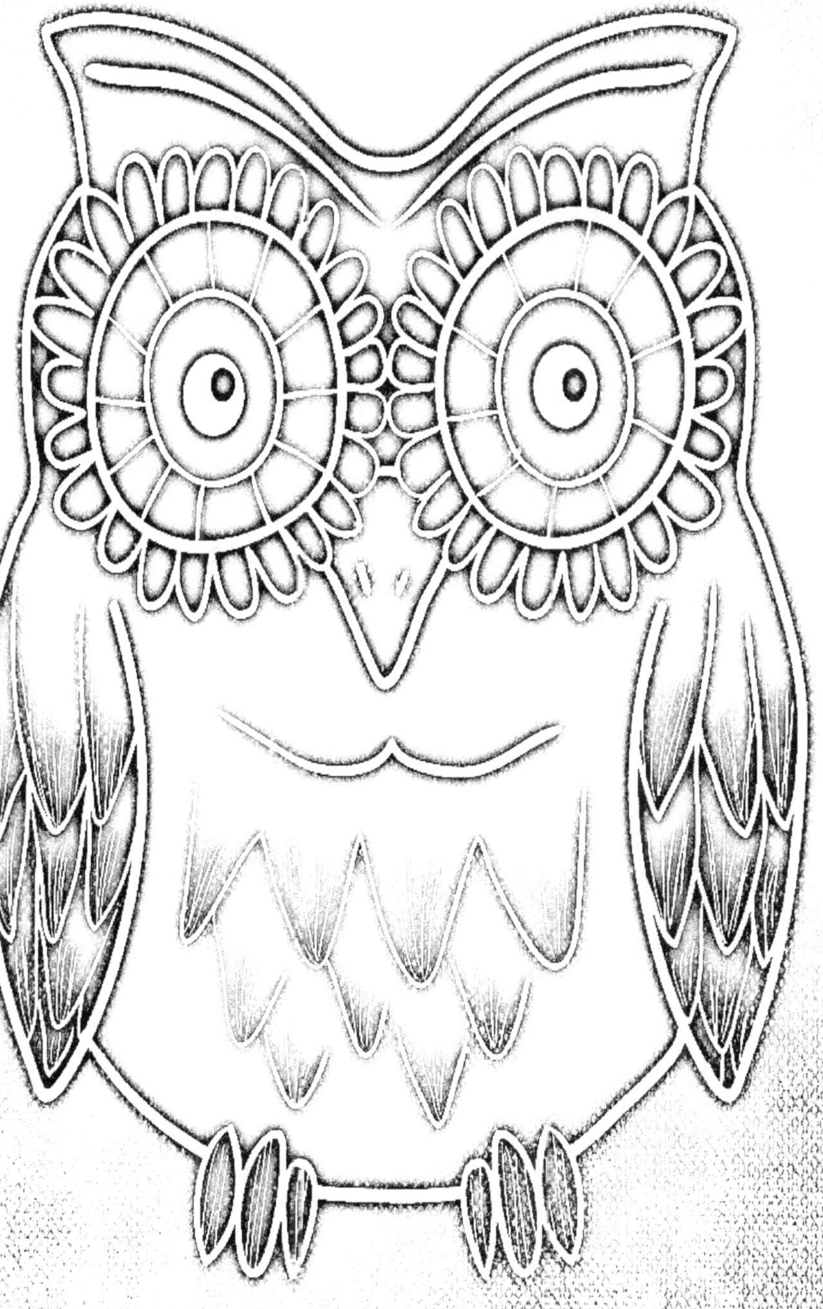

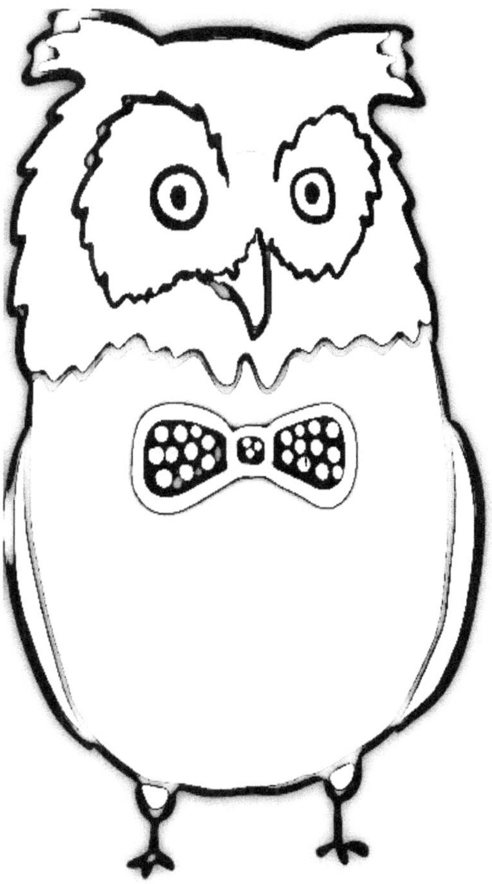

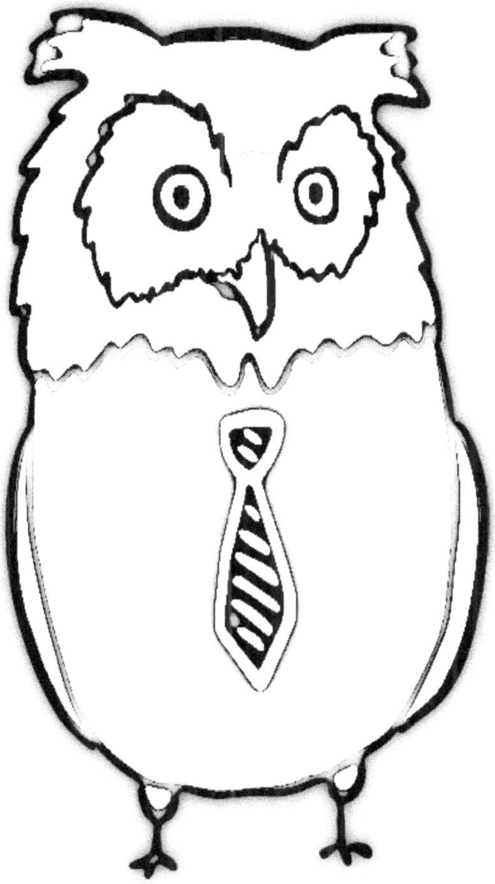

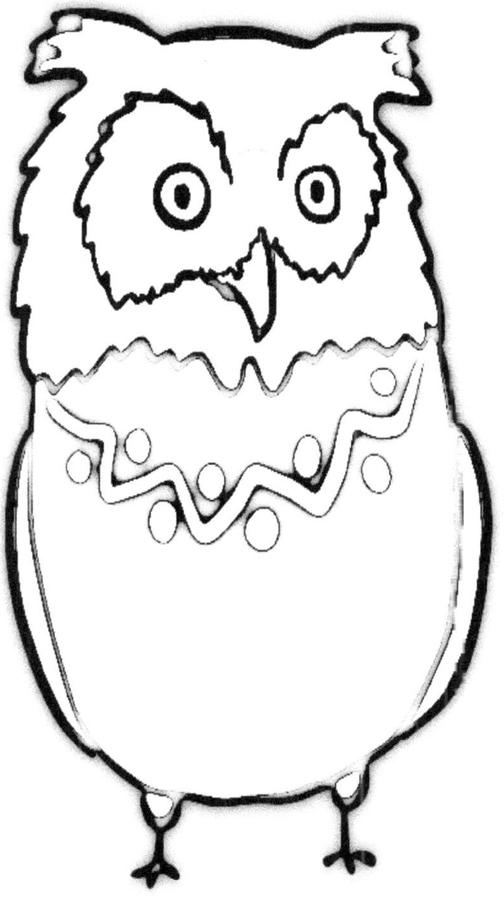

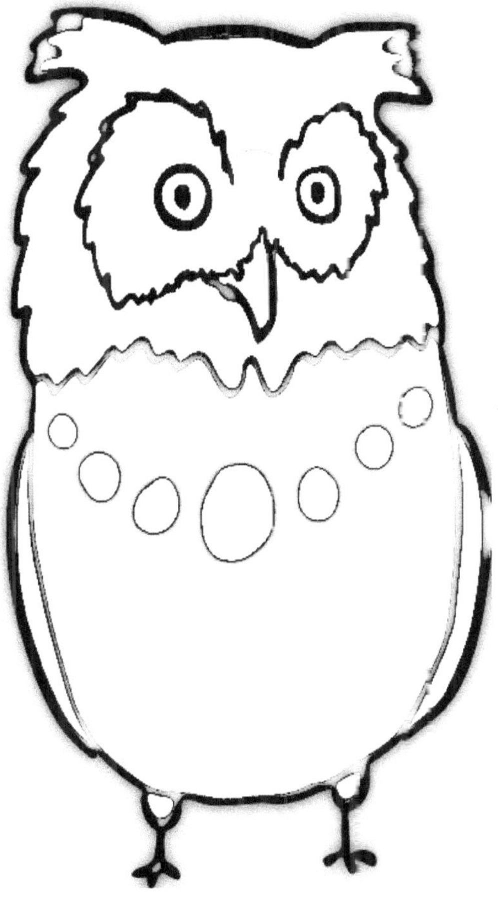

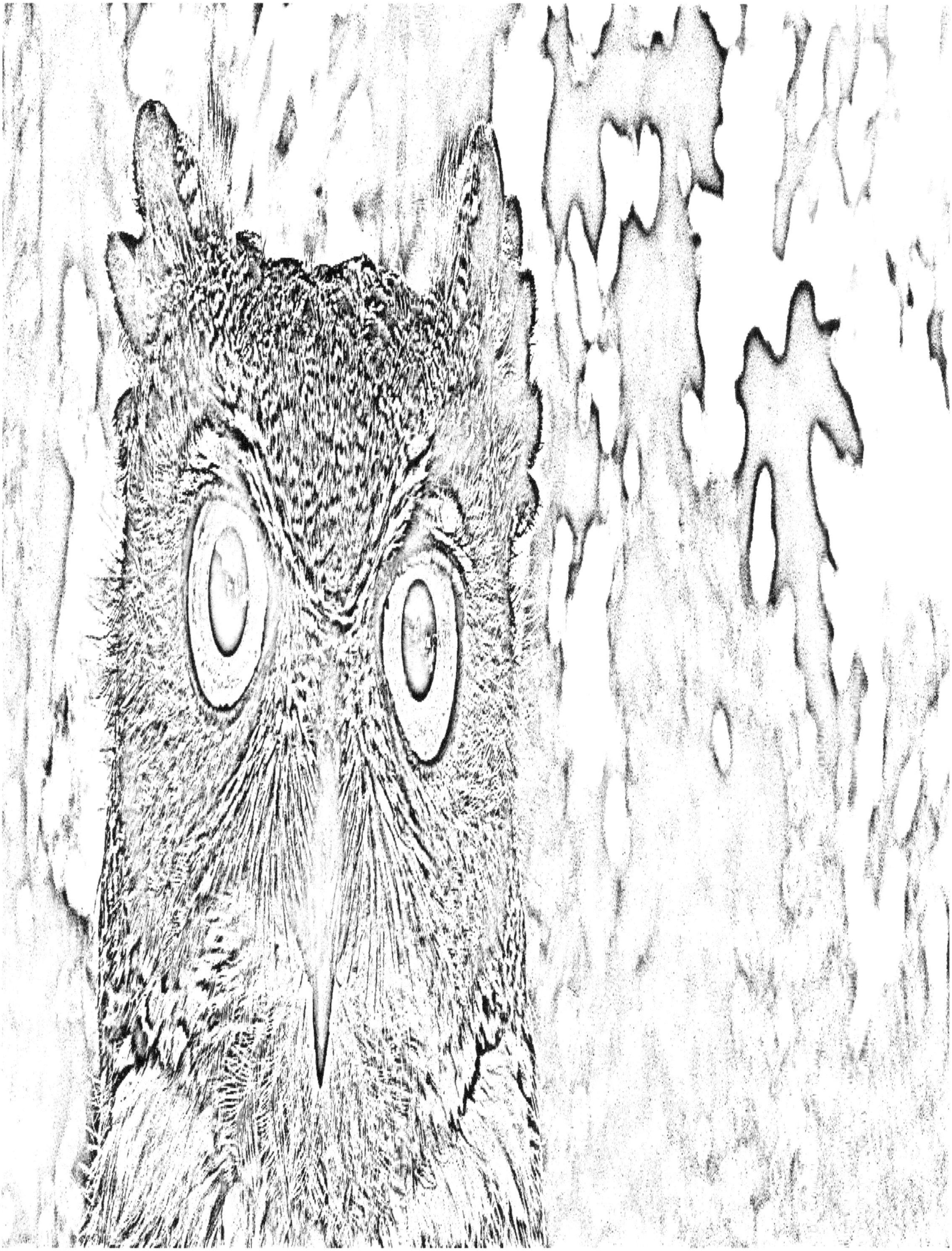

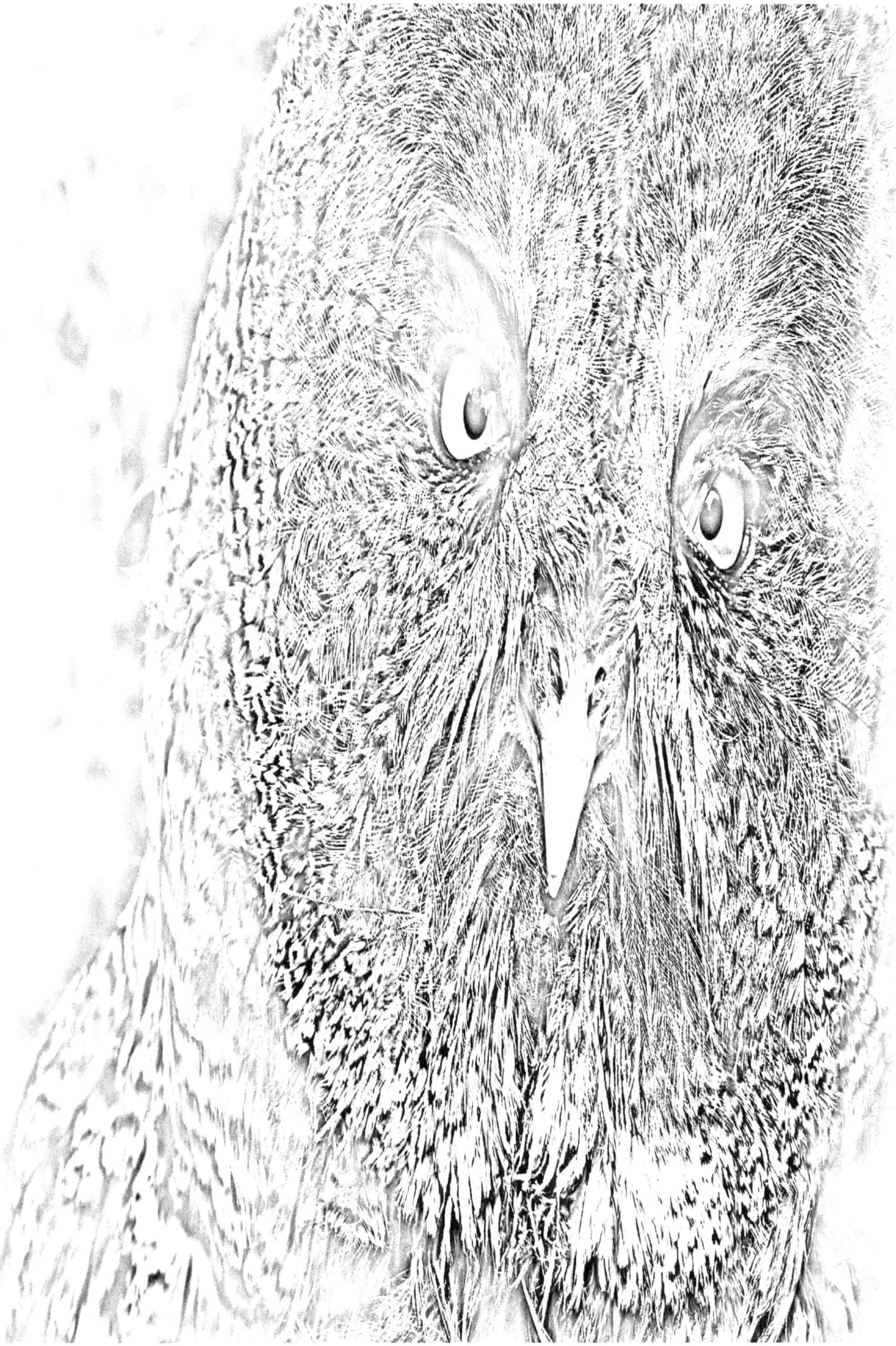

www.ingramcontent.com/pod-product-compliance
Lightning Source LLC
Chambersburg PA
CBHW081540280526
45788CB00010B/3311
* 9 7 8 1 5 3 0 8 8 5 8 6 2 *